Emotional LevelUp

A Teen's Guide to Riding the Wave (Without Wiping Out)

By
Jami May

Published by

Books N Ink Publishing
www.booksninkpublishing.com

Printed in the United States of America

Dedication

To my own teenagers, who taught me that feeling deeply is not a weakness but a profound courage.

And to every young person who has ever been told they feel too much—this is for you. Your feelings are not a burden; they are your superpower. This book is not a map to a fixed destination, but a compass to help you navigate your own path. Trust yourself. Find the strength within the storm. You are the expert on you, and you are never alone—ever!

Acknowledgment

A book about navigating emotions inevitably comes from a place of living them, and for that, my greatest teachers have been my family.

To my two incredible teens, this book exists because of you. Thank you for allowing me a front-row seat to the beautiful, complex, and honest journey of your lives. You have taught me more about resilience, authenticity, and the power of feeling than any textbook ever could. Watching you navigate your own storms with such courage has been my deepest inspiration. My greatest hope is that this book makes you feel seen, understood, and empowered in your journey.

To our family unit, thank you for the conversations around the dinner table, the shared struggles, the laughter that pulls us through, and the love that is our ultimate foundation. You are my heart, and this book is for you.

About the Author

Jami May is a mom of two teenagers who's in the thick of it, navigating high school drama, late-night talks, and the endless search for snacks. Writing under a pen name, she shares the lessons learned from her own beautiful, chaotic trenches, offering simple, down-to-earth tools to help teens handle the big feelings that come with growing up.

Jami believes you don't need to be a professional to offer a guiding hand—you just need honesty, compassion, and a little bit of humor. Her writing combines personal experience with a genuine understanding of teenage struggles, all with the goal of making mental health skills accessible and engaging.

At the end of the day, Jami just wants every teen to know they're not alone. She wrote this book for her own kids, and for yours, hoping to make the rollercoaster of teen life feel a little less bumpy and to show that it's more than okay to feel everything big, messy, and real.

A Note For You—The Reader

Hey. Welcome.

If you're holding this book (or scrolling through it), chances are you've felt something recently that was a lot. Maybe it was a frustration that made you want to scream into a pillow, a sadness that felt like a heavy blanket, an anxiety that tied your stomach in knots, or a joy so big you thought your heart might burst.

First things first: that is completely, 100% normal. Being a teen is like having the emotional volume knob turned all the way up. Everything is intense. Your brain is literally under construction, and your hormones are like uninvited party guests who keep messing with the music.

This book isn't about turning the volume down. It's not about shutting off your feelings. Your emotions are powerful, valuable, and they are trying to tell you something. This book is a toolkit. It's a guide to understanding those messages, learning to surf the big waves instead of being pulled under by them, and channeling that incredible energy into something positive.

You are not broken. You are under construction.

Let's build.

Table of Contents

CHAPTER
01
THE SCIENCE
OF THE FEELS

Chapter 1: What's Going On in There? The Science of the Feels

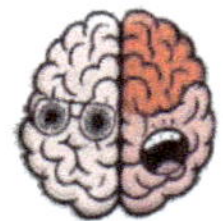

Before we talk about how to handle emotions, let's talk about why they feel so intense. Spoiler alert: it's not your fault.

Your Brain on Adolescence: Prefrontal Cortex vs. Amygdala

Imagine your brain has two main characters:

1. **The Amygdala:** This is your emotional alarm system. It's primal, fast, and reacts instantly to threats. It's the part that screams, "DANGER!" when you get a bad grade or someone looks at you funny.

2. **The Prefrontal Cortex:** This is the CEO of your brain. It's responsible for rational thought, decision-making, impulse control, and calming down the amygdala. It's the voice that says, "Okay, a bad grade isn't ideal, but let's make a plan to study for the next one."

Here's the kicker: during your teenage years, the amygdala is fully developed and super sensitive. But the prefrontal cortex? It's under construction until your mid-20s! So sometimes, the alarm system (amygdala) hijacks the construction site (prefrontal cortex). This is why you might react intensely first and think logically later.

Hormones: The Body's Chemical Messengers

Hormones like estrogen, progesterone, and testosterone are surging through your body. They're essential for physical growth, but they also deeply affect your mood and emotions. They can amplify everything,  making a small annoyance feel like a major catastrophe. It's like your emotional sound system has a really bad DJ.

Why Emotions Are Actually Your Superpower

Even though they can be overwhelming and uncomfortable, emotions are not the enemy. They are data, not glitches. They give you crucial information about your needs, your values, and your environment.

Your emotions aren't a glitch. They are your built-in, high-tech guidance system. They evolved over millions of years for one simple reason: they helped our ancestors survive. They are data points, flashing lights on your internal dashboard, each trying to send you a crucial message about your needs, your values, and your environment.

 Ignoring them is like ignoring the low battery on your phone. You can ignore it, but you'll still end up with a dead phone. Learning to understand them is like learning to speak the language of your deepest self.

Let's break down your core emotional "superpowers" and the vital intel they're trying to deliver:

1. **Anger: The Boundary Defender**

    What it feels like: Heat, tension, clenched jaw, frustration, rage.

    Its Superpower Message: "A boundary has been crossed! Something is unfair or unjust!"

    Why it's useful: Anger alerts you to a violation. It provides a burst of energy and courage to stand up for yourself, protect someone else, or fight for a cause you believe in. Without anger, you'd be a doormat, unable to defend your physical or emotional space. It's not about screaming or hitting; it's about hearing its message and using that energy to assertively say, "This is not okay."

2. **Sadness: The Signal for Healing**

    What it feels like: Heaviness, tears, lethargy, a hollow feeling.

    Its Superpower Message: "I have lost something important. I need to slow down and heal."

    Why it's useful: Sadness forces you to pause. It encourages you to withdraw, turn inward, and process a loss—whether it's the end of a friendship, a missed opportunity, or a change in your life. This slowing down is essential for integration and healing. It also signals to others that you need comfort and connection, strengthening social bonds. Sadness is the rain that allows for new growth.

3. **Fear: The Protector & Preparer**

    What it feels like: Butterflies, racing heart, hyper-vigilance, dread.

    Its Superpower Message: "Danger might be near! Get ready!"

    Why it's useful: Fear is your ultimate bodyguard. It sharpens your senses, pumps adrenaline to help you run faster or fight harder, and forces you to assess risk. In the modern world, the "danger" is rarely a saber-toothed tiger; it's an upcoming test, a social situation, or an uncertain future. Fear's job is to prepare you. It's not about paralyzing you; it's about making you alert and ready to perform.

4. **Joy: The GPS for Your Values**

    What it feels like: Lightness, laughter, warmth, energy, excitement.

    Its Superpower Message: "This is good! More of this, please!"

    Why it's useful: Joy is your internal compass. It connects you to what you love, what you value, and what gives your life meaning. It rewards you for positive connections, achievements, and experiences, encouraging you to seek them out again. Joy builds resilience, strengthens your immune system, and buffers you against stress. It's the fuel that keeps you going.

5. **Disgust: The Guardian of Your Values**

    What it feels like: Revulsion, nausea, a desire to pull away.

    Its Superpower Message: "This is toxic! Get away!"

Why it's useful: Disgust originally protected us from eating poisonous food or coming into contact with disease. Emotionally, it does the same thing. It helps you reject things that are morally wrong, harmful to your well-being, or just "not for you." It protects your values and your sense of self by making you say, "No, thanks," to people, situations, or ideas that feel wrong.

Thinking of emotions this way changes everything. The goal isn't to delete "negative" emotions from your emotional playlist. The goal is to become a skilled DJ of your own feelings.

A good DJ doesn't rip the headphones off when a song with a heavy bassline comes on. They listen, understand its rhythm and message, and then decide how to mix it, lower its volume, or let it play out so the next song can begin.

Your job is to do the same. Listen to the message. Thank your anger for protecting you. Honor your sadness for asking you to heal. Respect your fear for trying to keep you safe. And then, with the tools in this book, you decide what to do with that information.

Your emotions aren't your enemies. They are your oldest allies. They are your superpower. It's time to learn how to use them.

FRUSTRATION
CHAPTER
02
IDENTIFYING YOUR
EMOTIONS
EMOTION RADAR

Chapter 2: Meet the Crew: Identifying Your Emotions

We often lump feelings into "good" and "bad." But that's like saying all food is either "delicious" or "disgusting." There's a whole spectrum in between. Let's get specific.

The Big Five (and Their Many Cousins)

Most of our emotions are blends or intensities of a few core ones:

1. **Anger:**
   - **Annoyance:** A pebble in your shoe.
   - **Frustration:** Hitting a wall, again and again.
   - **Irritation:** Everything is grating on your nerves.
   - **Resentment:** Holding onto a past anger; a slow burn.
   - **Rage:** A full-blown wildfire of emotion.

2. **Sadness:**
   - **Disappointment:** Things didn't turn out as I'd hoped.

- **Hurt:** Feeling wounded by someone's words or actions.
- **Loneliness:** Aching for connection.
- **Shame:** The feeling that I am bad, not that I did something bad.
- **Grief:** The deep, profound sadness of a major loss.

3. **Fear:**

- **Anxiety:** Fear about a future, uncertain threat.
- **Worry:** Cycling thoughts about a problem.
- **Nervousness:** Butterflies before a big event.
- **Insecurity:** Fear of not being good enough.
- **Panic:** Sudden, overwhelming terror.

4. **Joy:**

- **Happiness:** General contentment.
- **Excitement:** Anticipatory joy.
- **Pride:** Joy in your own accomplishments.
- **Gratitude:** Joy, appreciation for someone or something.
- **Contentment:** A peaceful, quiet joy.

5. **Disgust:**

- **Distaste:** A mild dislike or aversion. (Example: Not liking the texture of a food.)

- **Dislike:** A feeling of distaste or hostility. A simple "nope."
- **Aversion:** Actively wanting to avoid something.
- **Contempt:** The feeling that a person or a thing is beneath consideration, worthless, or deserving of scorn. (This is a powerful blend of anger and disgust).
- **Revulsion:** An intense feeling of disgust and loathing. A powerful feeling of wanting to get away.
- **Repulsion:** The physical force of disgust; the urge to push something away.

The Body-Mind Connection: Where You Feel Emotions

Emotions aren't just in your head; you feel them in your body. Start noticing:

- Do you get a tight chest when you're anxious?
- Do your shoulders tense up when you're stressed?
- Does your stomach clench when you're angry?
- Do you feel light and warm when you're happy?

Your body is an emotion radar. Tuning into these physical signals helps you identify what you're feeling before it gets overwhelming.

CHAPTER
03
MINDFULNESS
& GROUNDING

Chapter 3: Tool #1
The Pause Button (Mindfulness & Grounding)

When a big emotion hits, your first instinct is often to react immediately. The Pause Button is the skill of creating a tiny space between the feeling and your action. In that space, you find your power to choose.

How to Hit ⏸ Pause Before You React

- Stop. Literally. Freeze for one second.
- Take one deep breath. In through your nose for 4 counts, out through your mouth for 6 counts. The long exhale tells your nervous system to calm down.
- Ask yourself: "What am I feeling right now?" Just naming it activates your prefrontal cortex.

The 5-4-3-2-1 Grounding Technique. When you feel overwhelmed or disconnected, this trick pulls you back into the present moment by engaging your senses. Name:

 • 5 things you can see (a lamp, a speck on the wall, a crack in your phone screen)

• 4 things you can feel (your feet on the floor, the fabric of your shirt, the chair against your back)

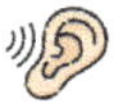 • 3 things you can hear (the hum of a fridge, a car outside, your own breathing)

 • 2 things you can smell (your laundry detergent, air

freshener, or just take a deep breath of the air)

 • 1 thing you can taste (the aftertaste of your last drink, or take a sip of water)

Simple Breathing Exercises That Actually Work

- **Box Breathing**: Breathe in for 4 counts, hold for 4, breathe out for 4, hold for 4. Repeat.
- **Belly Breathing**: Put a hand on your stomach. Breathe in deeply through your nose, feeling your belly push your hand out. Breathe out slowly through your mouth, feeling your hand go back in.

Word List
SAD
HAPPY
CRYING
???
CHAPTER
04
NAMING &
VALIDATING
I FEEL...
Expanding emotional vocabulary

Chapter 4: Tool #2
The Decoder Ring (Naming & Validating)

Once you've hit pause, you need to figure out what you're dealing with. "I feel bad" is too vague. Let's get specific.

Expanding Your Emotional Vocabulary

Instead of "I'm stressed," try to be more precise:

- "I feel overwhelmed because I have too much homework."
- "I feel unprepared for this test."
- "I feel pressured to do well."

Here's a trick: Use "I feel..." followed by an emotion word, not a thought. "I feel like you're ignoring me" is a thought. "I feel lonely" or "I feel ignored" is an emotion.

How to Validate Your Own Feelings

Validation is simply acknowledging that your feeling makes sense. It's saying to yourself:

- "Of course I feel anxious, I have a big presentation tomorrow."

- "It makes sense that I'm sad, that friendship meant a lot to me."
- "Anyone would feel frustrated in this situation."

This is NOT saying your reaction is perfect. It's just accepting that it's there. Fighting a feeling is like struggling in quicksand—it makes you sink faster. Acceptance is the first step to managing it.

Journaling Prompts to Unpack the Mess

- "When did this feeling start?"
- Where do you feel the emotion in your body?
- "What happened right before I felt this way?"
- What was the trigger? (A comment, a grade, a memory, a text message?) 
- "What is this emotion trying to tell me?
- What do I need right now?"
- What is one small, kind thing I can do right now to meet that need?

CHAPTER
05
HEALTHY
EXPRESSION

Chapter 5: Tool #3
The Pressure Valve (Healthy Expression)

You've hit pause. You've named the feeling: you're furious. Now what? That energy is still buzzing through you. You need to release it in a way that doesn't break anything.

Move It, Don't Brew It

Emotions get stored in your body. Release them physically:

- Go for a run or a fast walk.
- Do a workout, follow a yoga video, or dance like a maniac in your room.
- Squeeze a stress ball or punch a pillow.
- Shake it out. Literally shake your arms, legs, and whole body for 60 seconds.

Create Something

Transform the messy feeling into something tangible:

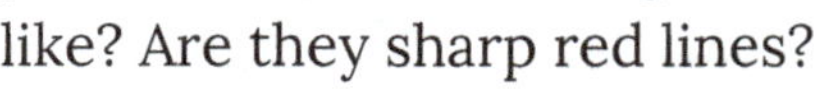

- Draw or paint it. What does anger look like? Are they sharp red lines?
- Write it out. Write a furious poem, a sad song, a letter you never sent.
- Play music. Put on a song that matches your mood and play air guitar.

Talk It Out (Wisely)

Sometimes, you need to vent. But choose your person carefully.

- Ask for permission: "Hey, I need to vent. Do you have space to listen?"
- Choose someone trustworthy, not someone who will fuel the drama.
- After you vent, try to pivot. "Thanks for listening. Want to watch a funny video?" This prevents you from just circling the drain of negativity.

Remember: The goal is release, not rumination. Expressing emotion isn't about creating a masterpiece or having a perfect workout. It's about honoring the energy inside you by giving it a respectful and constructive way to exit the building. By choosing your Pressure Valve, you take final, powerful control over the emotional **W.A.V.E.**, and you **R.I.D.E.** it all the way to shore.

R.I.D.E. the W.A.V.E. stands for:

Recognize the feeling rising.
Investigate it with curiosity.
Decode its message.
Express it safely.

Wait before you react.
Acknowledge the emotion.
Validate your experience.
Engage in a healthy outlet.

CHAPTER
06
NAVIGATING
SPECIFIC STORMS

Chapter 6: Navigating Specific Storms

Rage Mode: Anger & Frustration

- **Message:** A boundary has been crossed. Something is unfair.
- **Toolkit:** HIT PAUSE FIRST. Walk away. Use intense physical release (exercise). Once calm, use "I feel" statements to communicate what felt unfair. ("I felt disrespected when…")

The Heavy Blanket: Sadness & Grief

- **Message:** You've experienced a loss. You need comfort and time to heal.
- **Toolkit:** Let yourself feel it. Don't try to "just be happy." Watch a sad movie and cry it out. Talk to someone comforting. Be gentle with yourself. Do one small, kind thing for yourself (take a shower, make tea).

The Worry Loop: Anxiety & Overthinking

- Message: Your brain is trying to protect you from a future threat (real or imagined).
- Toolkit: Question the thought. "Is it true that the worst will happen?" Contain it. Give yourself a 10-minute

"worry period" later. Get present. Use the 5-4-3-2-1 grounding technique. Focus on what you can control.

The Green-Eyed Monster: Jealousy & Envy

- **Message:** You want something someone else has. It highlights a desire or insecurity.
- **Toolkit:** Unfollow or mute social media accounts that trigger this. Instead of stewing, ask yourself: "What can I learn from them?" or "What is one small step I can take toward my own goal?" Use it as motivation, not self-punishment.

The Emptiness: Boredom & Apathy

- **Message:** You're disengaged. You need stimulation, purpose, or rest.
- **Toolkit:** This is a sign you need to try something new. Read a book on a random topic. Go for a walk somewhere new. Listen to a new genre of music. Sometimes, it's a sign you're actually burned out and need genuine rest, not just more screen time.

CHAPTER
07
EMOTIONS IN
RELATIONSHIPS

Chapter 7: The Social World: Emotions in Relationships

Other people have big feelings too. Navigating that is a next-level skill.

Communicating How You Feel Without Starting Drama

Use the simple I.F.E. Statement:

- **"I feel** [emotion]...
- **...when** [specific situation, not a judgment]...
- **...because** I need [or because it makes me feel]."
- **Instead of:** "You never listen to me!" (accusation)
- **Try: "I feel** frustrated **when** I'm talking and the phone is out, **because** I need to feel heard."

Dealing with Other People's Big Emotions

You are not responsible for fixing other people's feelings. Your job is to be respectful.

- **Listen**. Often, people just want to be heard.
- **Validate**. "It sounds like you're really hurt. That makes sense."
- **Set a boundary if needed**. "I want to support you, but I can't help if you're yelling at me. Let's talk when we're both calm."

Setting Boundaries to Protect Your Energy

A boundary is a rule for how you allow others to treat you. It's not mean; it's necessary.

- "I'm not available to text after 10 PM."
- "I don't like jokes about my weight. Please don't make them."
- "I need some alone time to recharge right now."

CHAPTER
08
BUILDING YOUR
EMOTIONAL FITNESS
ROUTINE

Chapter 8: Building Your Emotional Fitness Routine

You wouldn't run a marathon without training. Don't expect to handle emotional marathons without training either.

Daily Habits for a More Balanced You

1. **Sleep:** This is non-negotiable. Your brain processes emotions while you sleep. Aim for 8-10 hours. 

 2. **Nutrition:** Food is fuel. Eating regular, balanced meals keeps your blood sugar stable, which keeps your moods stable.

3. **Movement:** Even a 15-minute walk can dramatically improve your mood by releasing endorphins.

Digital Detox: Managing Social Media Stress

1. Curate your feed. Unfollow accounts that make you feel bad about yourself.
2. Set time limits. Use your phone's settings to limit time on apps.
3. Charge your phone outside your bedroom, if possible. This improves sleep and reduces the urge to scroll mindlessly.

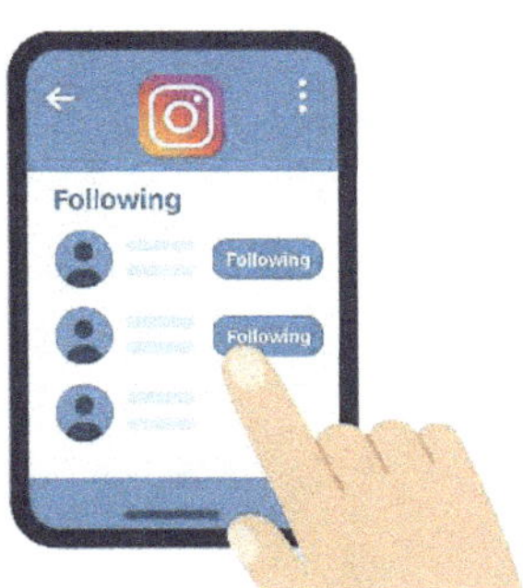

Cultivating Joy and Gratitude on Purpose

Your brain has a natural negativity bias. You have to consciously practice positivity.

- **Three Good Things:** Each night, write down three specific things that were good today, no matter how small.
- **Savoring:** When something good happens, pause and really soak it in for 10 seconds. "This is awesome."

CHAPTER
09
WHEN TO ASK
FOR BACKUP

Chapter 9: When to Ask for Backup

Sometimes, the tools in this book aren't enough, and that's okay. Asking for help is a sign of incredible strength and self-awareness.

Signs It Might Be More Than Just a Bad Day

- Your emotions feel uncontrollable all the time, most of the day.
- You've lost interest in things you used to love.
- Your sleep or appetite has changed dramatically (too much or too little).
- You have thoughts of harming yourself or others.
- You're using substances to cope with or numb your feelings.

How to Talk to a Parent, Guardian, or Counselor

Starting the conversation is the hardest part.

1. Pick a calm time. Not in the middle of an argument.
2. Plan what to say:
   - "I haven't been feeling like myself lately."
   - "I'm struggling with my mood, and I think I need some help."
   - "Can I talk to you about something that's been

bothering me?"

3. If the first adult doesn't listen, try another. A school counselor, coach, doctor, or a friend's parent are all great options.

Putting It All Together
A Real-Life Example

Situation: Your friend makes a joke about your new haircut in front of a group, and everyone laughs.

1. **Pause Button:** You feel a hot flush. You take a deep breath instead of snapping back.
2. **Decoder Ring:** You check in. The primary feeling is anger (hot face, clenched jaw). The more specific feeling is humiliation (feeling disrespected and laughed at). Underneath, you might also feel a little hurt and sad.
3. **Validation:** You think, "It makes complete sense that I feel humiliated. Being laughed at in front of people is a really uncomfortable experience. Anyone would feel this way."
4. **Identify the Need:** The feeling is telling you your need for respect wasn't met. Your need is to re-establish that boundary.
5. **Action (or Expression):** Later, you might pull your friend aside and use an I-statement: "I felt really embarrassed when you joked about my hair in front of everyone. I'd appreciate it if you kept those comments for when it's just us."

Resources and Helplines
(You Are Not Alone)

Crisis Support:
1. 988 Suicide & Crisis Lifeline: Call or text 988 (in the US and Canada)
2. Crisis Text Line: Text HOME to 741741
3. The Trevor Project (LGBTQ+ Support): Call 1-866-488-7386 or text START to 678-678

General Support & Information:
1. Teen Line: Call 1-800-852-8336 or text TEEN to 839863
2. National Alliance on Mental Illness (NAMI): nami.org
3. The Jed Foundation: jedfoundation.org (mental health resources for teens and young adults)

Remember

You are capable, you are resilient, and you are not alone on this journey. Now go build your surfboard, surf life, and enjoy it all.